BELAIR
ACTIVE SCIENCE 6

Patricia Young

Contents

Belair
Publications

First published in 2000 by Belair Publications.
Apex Business Centre, Boscombe Road, Dunstable, LU5 4RL.
Email: belair@belair-publications.co.uk

Editor: Hayley Willer
Layout artist: Suzanne Ward
Illustrations: Bob Farley (Graham-Cameron Illustration)
Cover design: Martin Cross

© 2000 Belair Publications, on behalf of the author.
Reprinted 2001.

British Library Cataloguing in Publication Data. A catalogue record for this publication is available from the British Library.

ISBN 1 84191 075-9

Introduction

What is Active Science?

Active Science is a series of six books designed to be used with children aged five to eleven. The series provides teachers' notes and activity sheets matched to the topics in the QCA Scheme of Work for Science.

The activities included in the book are varied and challenging and encourage the children to think scientifically. The emphasis is on providing the children with first-hand experience of scientific practical work and investigation.

Active Science 6 can be used alongside the QCA Scheme as the basis of a year's work or it can be used to supplement existing schemes of work already in place in school.

The book is divided into twelve chapters. Each chapter consists of a teachers' page and three photocopiable activity sheets.

What is on the teachers' page?

- **Background** – This provides the necessary background knowledge for teachers to deliver the topic. This is not information that the children are required to know necessarily, but information to aid the teacher.

- **Activity pages** – This section contains:
  - the main learning objectives in terms of knowledge, understanding and skills, for each activity, to help teachers with planning and assessment
  - ideas for further activities
  - guidance points for discussion
  - safety warnings.

- **Oral work** – This section provides opportunities for:
  - discussion
  - questioning that encourages the children to think about the scientific process
  - oral presentations
  - interviewing
  - inviting guest speakers into the classroom
  - role-play.

- **Written work** – This section provides ideas for written work, including:
  - comparing and contrasting
  - producing leaflets and guides on certain scientific issues
  - planning investigations
  - writing conclusions and explanations
  - full scientific report writing.

- **ICT** – A range of opportunities for the use of ICT in the Science Curriculum is provided, including:
  - researching information using CD-ROM and the Internet
  - using ICT programs to produce scientific information in the form of text and graphics
  - using computer databases
  - using data-handling packages to present results of experiments
  - using audiotapes and videotapes to record work.

What about the activity pages?

The photocopiable activity sheets contain a variety of activities that provide opportunities for the children to do the following.

- **Plan** – This includes:
  - making predictions
  - considering what evidence is to be collected
  - planning investigations and fair tests.

- **Obtain and present evidence** – This includes:
  - making careful observations and measurements
  - using simple apparatus
  - choosing methods of recording
  - recording results systematically.

- **Consider evidence and evaluate** – This includes:
  - making comparisons
  - using results to draw conclusions
  - explaining in terms of scientific knowledge and understanding
  - considering whether a test is fair or not
  - deciding how an investigation could be improved.

Interdependence

Background

Green plants are able to convert energy into food. They need water, carbon dioxide from the air, and light to do this. Most of the food is made in the leaves.

Food chains always begin with a plant (a producer). This is because it is only plants that can produce their own food. Animals are called consumers because they consume food. Consumers in a pond can be divided into carnivores (eat live animals only), herbivores (eat plants only), omnivores (eat plants and animals) and scavengers/detrivores (eat dead plants and animals).

Activity pages

How Much Light?

Learning objectives
- To make careful observations and measurements.
- To know that plants will grow more healthily in light conditions.

The children will need to have germinated seeds before starting the investigation. Bean plants will be good to observe.

The children will need to keep the amount of water the same in each case. The plant with the least light will probably grow the tallest because it will be searching for access to light. However, it will look the least healthy; it may look yellow and spindly and have fewer leaves.

Identification of Pond Life

Learning objectives
- To be able to identify pond animals using a key.

This activity could be used as a preparation for the children before carrying out a pond study. They could observe animals to find out whether they eat animals or plants or both.

Answers to identification of animals

1	Water boatman	4	Caddis fly larva
2	Water flea	5	Diving beetle
3	Freshwater shrimp	6	Water snail

Food Webs in the Pond

Learning objectives
- To understand that animals and plants in a local environment are interdependent.

The children will need to draw some of the animals using the 'Identification of Pond Life' activity sheet.

Producers	Herbivores	Carnivores	Scavengers
Algae Plants	Water snail Water flea Lesser water boatman	Diving beetle Dragonfly larva	Freshwater shrimp Tadpole

If more beetles were introduced to the pond the number of tadpoles would reduce. Eventually, there would not be enough food for the beetles and dragonfly larvae. They would die. The freshwater shrimp would have an ample supply of food and its numbers would increase.

If all the beetles left the pond, the number of tadpoles would increase. This would provide more food for the dragonfly larvae so their numbers would increase.

Oral work

Ask the children how plants adapt so that they obtain as much light as possible. They may suggest that the leaves be positioned so that each leaf faces the Sun. Some plants change direction throughout the day so that they face the Sun for as long as possible (e.g. sunflowers). Variegated plants will turn greener in darker places but will become more variegated in light conditions.

Written work

Ask the children to produce a menu for a pond animal's dinner party.

Ask the children to imagine that they are pond animals and to write a letter of complaint to the beetles about their aggressive behaviour and the effect it is having on the local community.

ICT

Use video to show time-lapse pictures of growth of plants.

How Much Light?

Key Idea

The amount of light affects the growth of plants.

1. Carry out an investigation to see whether the amount of light affects the growth of plants.

Think about:

– What variables you will need to keep the same.
– What you will measure.
– Where you will place the plants so that they each get a different amount of light.

Measure the height of each plant every day and write notes or draw the plants.

2. Record your results in a table like the one below.

Day	Height of plant			
	Least light	**Some light**	**Most light**	**Any observations**
1				
2				
3				
4				
5				
6				
7				

3. How did you make it a fair test?

4. Which plant grew the most?

5. Which plant looked the healthiest?

6. Which plant looked the least healthy?

7. What do you think happened to each of the plants?

NOW Find a plant that is growing in a dark place. How do you think that it stays healthy?

Identification of Pond Life

Key Idea — Animals can be identified using a branching key.

● Ponds can contain many different animals. Use the key to identify and label the following.

① _____

② _____

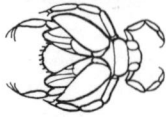

③ _____

④ _____

⑤ _____

⑥ _____

Does it have a shell?

Yes → **Water snail**

No → **Does it live in a tube?**

Yes → **Caddis fly larva**

No → **Has it four or more pairs of legs?**

Yes → **Freshwater shrimp**

No → **Has it wings?**

Yes → **Has it hard wing cases?**

No → **Water flea**

Has it hard wing cases?

Yes → **Diving beetle**

No → **Water boatman**

Food Webs in the Pond

Key Idea

Herbivores eat plants only, carnivores eat live plants only and scavengers eat dead plants and animals.

● A class of children observed some pond animals to find out what they eat. Here is a table of their results.

Animal	What it eats
Lesser water boatman	Algae
Diving beetle	Tadpoles, small fish and other insects
Freshwater shrimp	Dead organisms
Dragonfly larva	Tadpoles, water fleas and mayfly nymphs
Water snail	Thin layer of algae that grows on rocks and plants
Caddis fly larva	Plants and animals
Water flea	Tiny plants
Tadpole	Plants and dead animals

1. Look at the table above:

   a. Underline in green all the producers. Producers make their own food.

   b. What word describes all the other living things?

   c. Herbivores eat plants only. Underline in yellow all the herbivores.

   d. Carnivores eat live animals only. Underline in red all the carnivores.

   e. Scavengers eat dead plants and animals. Underline in blue all the scavengers.

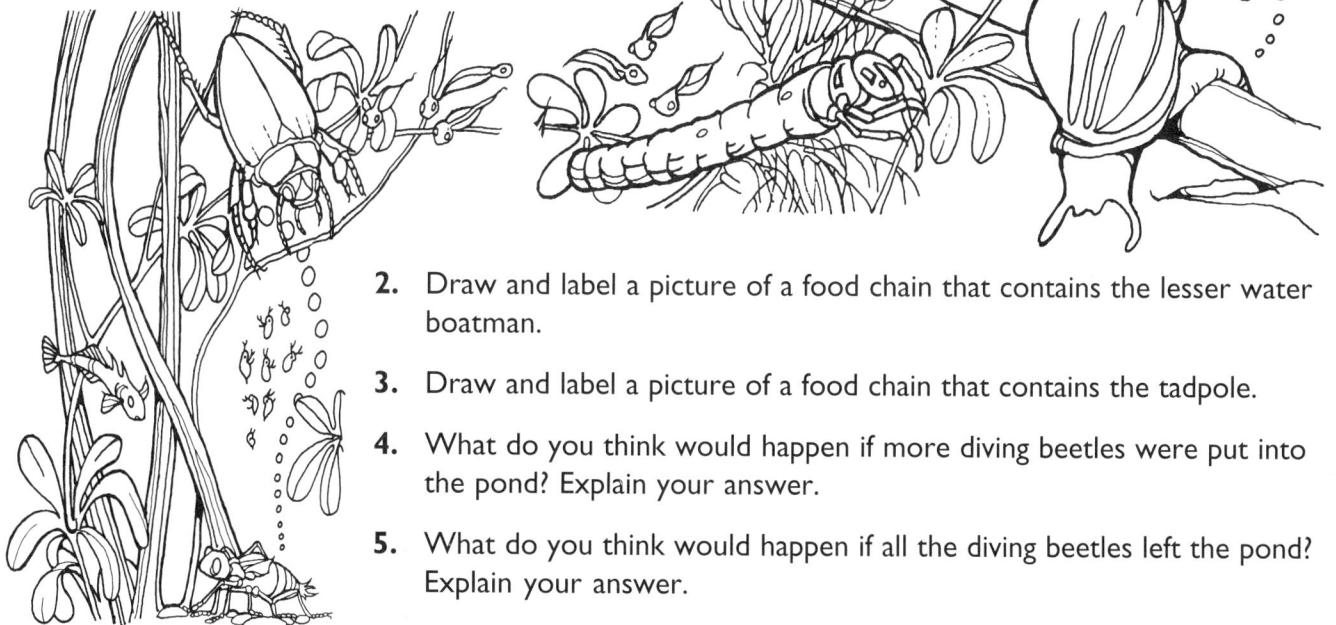

2. Draw and label a picture of a food chain that contains the lesser water boatman.

3. Draw and label a picture of a food chain that contains the tadpole.

4. What do you think would happen if more diving beetles were put into the pond? Explain your answer.

5. What do you think would happen if all the diving beetles left the pond? Explain your answer.

Adaptation

Background

Animals and plants have adapted so that they are suited to their environment. There are many different forms of living things that have evolved so that they can survive in a particular environment. Some have adapted by changing shape, some by adapting to certain conditions (e.g. cacti have evolved to survive in hot, dry conditions). Adaptations take place over many generations so that the animal or plant is most likely to survive and reproduce. This is the basis of Darwin's theory of evolution.

Activity pages

Looking at Walls

Learning objectives
- To make careful observations.
- To understand that walls are habitats for a variety of species.

This activity is best done on two contrasting walls, particularly if one is rural and the other urban. If this is not possible the children could observe different sides of the same wall. The children will need to discriminate between the species suggested. Algae are rather like powder. Lichen is either flat, crusty and crumbly or scaly, flat and leaf-like. The type of lichen will reflect the air quality; the bushier the leaf the cleaner the air. Mosses break down the surface of a wall, forming humus for other plants to grow on. Ferns will be found in the mortar or between the stones. There are a variety of flowering plants capable of growing on walls. The children may be able to identify the more common ones (e.g. ivy).

Adapted for Feeding

Learning objectives
- To interpret information.
- To understand that birds' beaks are adapted to their diet.

Birds use their beaks to catch or pick up food and to crush or tear it. Seed-eating birds usually have short, stout beaks so that they can crush the seeds. Insect-eating birds have slender beaks or wide, open beaks for scooping up insects while in flight. Flesh eaters have sharp, hooked beaks for tearing up flesh.

Answers to bird identifications:
1c, **2d**, **3h**, **4a**, **5g**, **6f**, **7b**, **8e**.

Adapted to Survive

Learning objectives
- To understand that animals and plants are adapted to their environment.

Here are possible answers to the table.

Adaptation	Reason
Plants have long roots.	To search for water deep underground.
Stems are covered in wax.	Reduces water loss.
Plants have small leaves or spines.	Reduces water loss.
Some animals have large ears.	Helps to remove heat.
Some animals have long tails.	Helps to remove heat.
Some animals are the same colour as their environment.	Helps predators and prey to be camouflaged.
Some animals can burrow.	Cooler under the ground during the day.
Some animals have long hair.	Keeps the heat off the animal.
Some animals sleep during the day.	To stay out of the sun and high temperatures.
Some animals' feet are splayed out (e.g. antelope).	To stop animal sinking into the sand.

Adaptations in cold climates could include: thick fur, colour, short ears and tail, hibernation.

Oral work

Discuss how other animals' mouths and teeth are adapted to their diet (e.g. rabbit, snake).

Written work

Ask the children to research how animals from different climates are adapted.

ICT

The children could create a database of plants that grow on walls.

Looking at Walls

You will need

– Pictures of algae, lichens, mosses, ferns, flowering plants

Key Idea Different plants grow in different habitats.

● What grows on or near a wall depends on many factors. This activity will ask you to look at the factors that may be important when looking at growth on walls. The best walls to study are old ones that have had more opportunity to develop growth. You may, however, find growth on new walls too.

1. Look at some pictures of different kinds of plant growth that may appear on walls and make sure you know the difference between them.

2. Choose two walls in different conditions and answer the following questions for each.

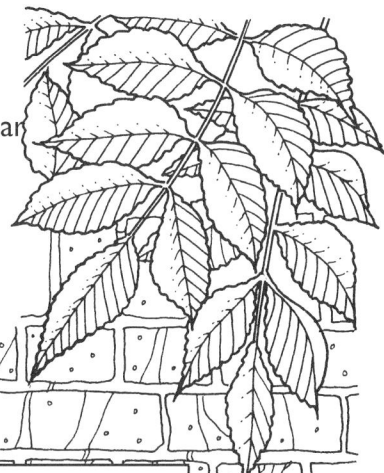

	Wall 1	Wall 2
What is the wall made of?		
Does it face the Sun?		
Is it shaded by overhanging trees?		
Is it exposed to the wind?		
What grows at the top of the wall?		
What grows in the mortar?		
What grows on the brickwork or stonework?		
What grows at the base of the wall?		

3. What is the same about the two walls?

NOW Can you find another wall that has the same growth as one of the walls you have studied?

Adapted for Feeding

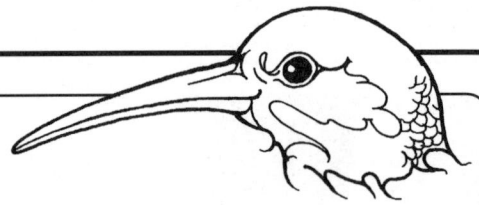

Key Idea

Birds' beaks are adapted to their diet.

1. Match each bird to the correct description of its beak and diet.

① The owl has a large hooked beak although some of it is buried in its feathers. The owl eats mice and other small animals.

② The curlew has a long, narrow beak that curves downwards. It walks along the shore and eats worms and shellfish.

③ The turnstone has a short but strong bill. It lives near the shore and turns over stones to find shellfish and shrimps.

④ The parrot has a short beak. The top part of its beak is curved over the lower half. It eats nuts and seeds.

⑤ The toucan lives in tropical forests. It has a large beak and eats juicy fruit.

⑥ The kingfisher has a large straight beak. It swallows fish whole.

⑦ The mallard duck lives in shallow water and feeds on water plants.

⑧ The swallow has a small bill. It catches insects while in flight.

a.

b.

c.

d.

e.

f.

g.

h.

2. For each of the birds, explain how the beak is adapted to the bird's diet.

3. Find diagrams of other birds and write about how their beaks are adapted to their diet.

NOW   Find out how human teeth are adapted to their diet.

Adapted to Survive

Key Idea	Animals and plants are adapted to their environment.

1. The Sahara desert is hot and dry. The animals and plants that live there are specially adapted. Here are some adaptations of some of the plants and animals. Explain why each adaptation will help the animal or plant to survive in the desert.

Adaptation	Reason
Plants have long roots.	
Stems are covered in wax.	
Plants have small leaves or spines.	
Some animals have large ears.	
Some animals have long tails.	
Some animals are the same colour as their environment.	
Some animals can burrow.	
Some animals have long hair.	
Some animals sleep during the day.	
Some animals' feet are splayed out (e.g. antelope).	

2. Research the animal and plant life that is found in very cold climates. How have they adapted to their environment? Make a table like the one you have completed.

NOW Imagine that you have discovered a very hot, wet part of the Earth's surface where there are plants and animals that have never been seen before. Draw an imaginary animal that might live there. Describe how it has adapted to survive in this environment.

Micro-organisms

Micro-organisms are living organisms that are neither animal nor plant and that are too small to be seen with the naked eye. Some are used in the food industry to make bread, cheese, yoghurt and beer. Some are responsible for the decay of dead organisms and the creation of humus in the soil. Some micro-organisms are also responsible for diseases in animals and plants. Viruses and bacteria are micro-organisms.

Activity pages

Yeast and Bread

Learning objectives
- To know that yeast is a living organism.
- To investigate what yeast needs to grow and reproduce.

Yeast is a single-celled fungus that must absorb sugar and requires moisture and warmth if it is to grow and reproduce. Fresh yeast can be obtained from health food stores. If dried yeast is used the process will take longer. When added to sugar solution, the yeast will respire and produce carbon dioxide. This will inflate a balloon. If the mixture is left in a cold place (e.g. refrigerator) then respiration will not take place. The best temperature for yeast to work is about 35°C. If boiling water is added to the yeast then it will be killed. Do not add too much sugar to the yeast as it will draw water from the yeast causing it to become dehydrated and it will finally die.

Adding either salt or sugar to food stuffs will help to preserve them. Salt and sugar draw water from mould or bacteria causing dehydration and death of the cells.

Safety: Some children may be allergic to yeast. Check before you introduce this organism to them.

Rotting Away

Learning objectives
- To observe changes in food.
- To interpret findings.

Some of the processed food will turn mouldy (e.g. bread, cheese) while some will turn brown and rot (e.g. apples). Microbes in the air affect all foodstuffs eventually. However, the microbes prefer a warm, damp environment so foods containing water will change first. Packaging food helps to keep the microbes away or does not allow the microbes to grow. Foods may be unsafe to eat long before you can see any signs of rotting. Some dried foods taste unpleasant when they have not been stored properly. This is because they have either lost moisture or absorbed water from the air. As an additional activity the children could plan an investigation to find out if cakes or biscuits lose moisture when left uncovered.

Safety – Do not allow the children to take the lids off the containers.

Staying Healthy

Learning objectives
- To understand that micro-organisms cause disease.
- To understand that a body well looked after is less likely to become diseased.

Some things we should do to help us to stay healthy are: keep flies away from food, keep raw meat separate from cooked meat, thoroughly thaw frozen meat before cooking, wash hands before touching any food, thoroughly cook eggs, maintain a balanced diet, avoid too much stress, treat any disease in its early stages, make sure the classroom is well ventilated.

Oral work

Discuss what happens at each stage of the bread-making process. The yeast takes time to grow and reproduce. As it respires, gas is given off. It is this gas that makes the bread rise.

Written work

The children could research different diseases or the development of various vaccines (e.g. the smallpox vaccine developed by Edward Jenner).

ICT

Use a digital camera to record the rotting foodstuffs. Sequences of pictures can then be retained for future reference.

Yeast and Bread

Yeast is a living organism.

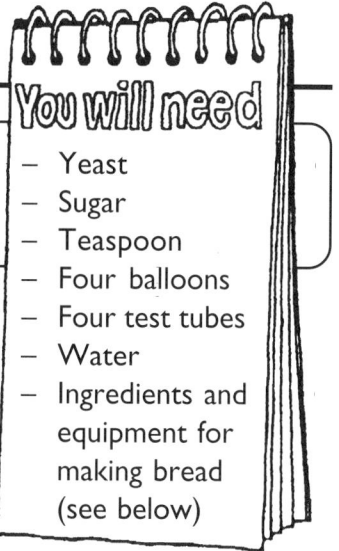

● All living things feed, respire and reproduce. This activity will help you to see what happens to yeast if it is given some food.

1. Put half a teaspoonful of yeast into each of two test tubes.
   Add one teaspoonful of sugar and six teaspoonfuls of warm water to one of the test tubes.
   Put a balloon over the end of each of the test tubes.
   Leave them both for 30 minutes in a warm place.

2. Observe what has happened in each of the test tubes and explain why you think there is a difference between them.

3. a. What do you think would happen if you put only yeast and sugar in a test tube?
   b. What do you think would happen if you put only yeast and water in a test tube?
   c. Do an experiment to see if you are correct.

Test tube 1   Test tube 2

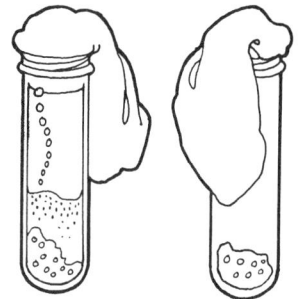

4. a. Make your own bread by following the recipe below.

   200g plain flour
   2g fresh yeast
   $\frac{1}{2}$ teaspoon salt
   $\frac{1}{2}$ teaspoon sugar
   120ml warm water

   Mix the flour and salt.
   Mix the yeast, sugar and one teaspoon water.
   Add the yeast, sugar and water to the flour.
   Mix with your hands until a thick dough is formed.
   Knead on a floured board for ten minutes.
   Cover with a damp cloth.
   Leave in a warm place for one hour.
   Knead the dough on a floured board for five minutes.
   Put on a greased oven tray.
   Bake in an oven at 230°C (450°F or Gas mark 7) for 20 minutes.

   b. What do you think would happen if you left the salt out of your recipe for bread?
   c. What do you think would happen if you left out the yeast?
   d. What do you think would happen if you left out the sugar?
   e. Explain what is happening when the dough is left in a warm place for one hour.

Rotting Away

Key Idea   Different foods rot at different rates. Foods are packaged so that they can be stored for longer.

You will need
- Screw-top plastic bottles
- Selection of fruit and vegetables
- Bread
- Cheese
- Hard-boiled egg
- Cornflake
- Biscuit
- Cake
- Crisp

1. Put a small piece of each food into screw-top plastic bottles.
   Screw the tops on and tape them in place so that no one can accidentally open them.
   Observe each food and record your observations. (Think about the best way you can do this.)
   Predict what you think will have happened to each of them after one month.
   Leave the bottles in a safe place and observe the contents each week for four weeks.
   Record your observations.

2. Which food rotted most quickly?

3. Which food appeared to change most slowly?

4. Why do you think food 'goes off'?

5. What could you do to try to prevent each of the foods you observed from rotting?

6. How else do you think the foods might be changing?

7. On most packaged foods there is a date before which the food should be eaten.
   Find some examples and copy and complete the table below.

Type of foodstuff	'Use by' or 'Best before' date
Packet of crisps	Best before 05 August 2001

8. Which type of packaging keeps food edible the longest?

NOW   Can you find any foods that do not have a suggested use-by date?

Staying Healthy

Diseases can be caused when micro-organisms enter the body. Micro-organisms that cause diseases are called germs. Germs are either bacteria or viruses.

1. Read the following.

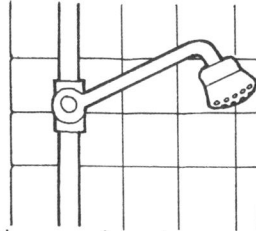

Germs can get into the body through the mouth and nose or through the skin, especially through cuts. Germs can spread by air, contaminated food or water and by contact with another person or animal. Our bodies have their own defence system. Good diet, exercise and plenty of rest help the defence system to work properly. Smoking, poor diet and drugs damage the defence system. Sometimes people are vaccinated against diseases; you may have been vaccinated against tuberculosis, polio and German measles.

Our bodies are adapted to reduce the number of germs that can get in. Our nose has hairs and mucus that help to trap dirt and germs. The dead outer layer of our skin forms a barrier to germs. Glands in the skin make a liquid that kills germs. A scab forms over a cut. This stops germs getting into the blood. Our tear glands make a liquid that kills germs. When we blink we spread the liquid over our eyes. There is a strong acid in our stomach that helps to kill many bacteria in our food.

Sometimes our bodies do not kill all the germs and this is when we become ill. There are things we can do that may stop us from becoming ill. Here are some ideas to start with.
- Wash your hands after going to the toilet and before a meal.
- Keep meat in the fridge.
- Wash kitchen work surfaces before food preparation.

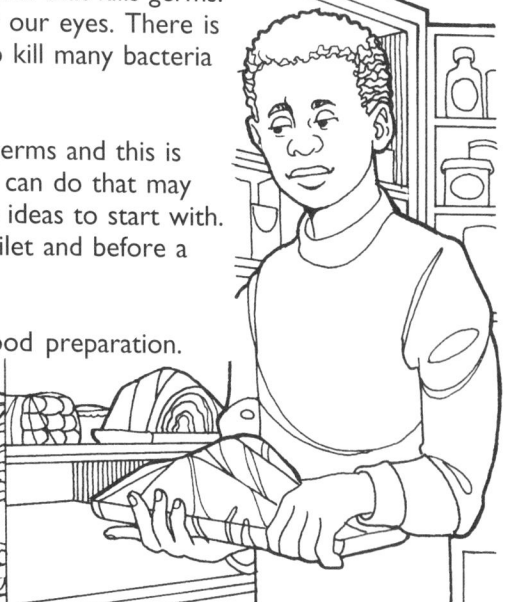

CLEANER ANTI BACTERIAL

2. Give a reason why each of the three actions above may help to keep you healthy.

3. Make a list of six other things we should do to help us to stay healthy.

NOW

Design a poster to explain to other children ways in which they should try to stay free of illnesses.

Solutions

A solution consists of a solvent and a solute. The solvent used in the activities in this section is water and the solutes are solids that are easily found in the home. There are other solvents including alcohol and dry-cleaning fluid. A solution is concentrated if there is a lot of solute in it. There is only so much solid that can dissolve in a set amount of liquid. When this amount has been reached the solution is called saturated. If more solid is added it will not dissolve. If a solution is left to evaporate, the solid will be left behind. Bottled water and tap water contain some solids although they are so small and are present in such small quantities that they will probably not be detected if water is left to evaporate.

Activity pages

Left Behind

Learning objectives
- To interpret results.
- To know that a solid is left behind if a liquid is allowed to evaporate from a solution.

The children could test a variety of liquids including sea, river and pond water. Each will probably contain some dissolved substances that should be left behind when the water has evaporated. The children are asked to think of the quickest way to evaporate the liquid. Safe suggestions might include: leave it in the sun, place on a plate warmer or on a hot water bottle.

Disappearing Sugar

Learning objectives
- To plan a fair test.
- To draw and interpret graphs.

Ensure that the children draw an appropriate graph. A bar chart should be drawn if discrete variables are used (e.g. types of sugar) and a line graph should be drawn if continuous data is used (e.g. temperature of water, amount of sugar or number of stirs).

Safety – If the children are considering the temperature of water, make sure they are supervised when using water above 50°C.

Solubility

Learning objectives
- To draw and extrapolate graphs.
- To understand that different masses of different solids dissolve in the same volume of water.
- To understand that different masses of solid dissolve at different temperatures.

The solubility of powder 3 is so great when the temperature is higher than 60°C that it would have taken too much to measure. The children should have continued the graph so that the following approximate values are given if the temperature had been 0°C.

White Powder (1)	8g
White Powder (2)	39g
White Powder (3)	15g
Blue powder	18g

Oral work

Explain to the children the terms 'soluble', 'dissolve', 'saturated'.

Question the children about the graphs from the dissolving sugar activity (e.g. 'What can you say about .... ?' or 'What makes you say that?').

Written work

Ask the children to write a poem about how water can cause things to disappear.

ICT

Children could record their results from the activity sheets 'Left Behind' and 'Disappearing Sugar' using a spreadsheet.

Left Behind

If a liquid is left to evaporate from a solution then a solid is left behind.

You will need

- 20ml of each of the following solutions:
  tap water
  salt water
  sugar in water
  dissolved coffee
  milk
  paint
  ink

1. Predict what will happen if you leave each of the solutions to evaporate.

2. How could you make the liquids evaporate as quickly as possible?

3. a. Carry out your investigation by leaving each of the solutions to evaporate. Were your predictions correct?
   b. Explain what has happened to each solution.

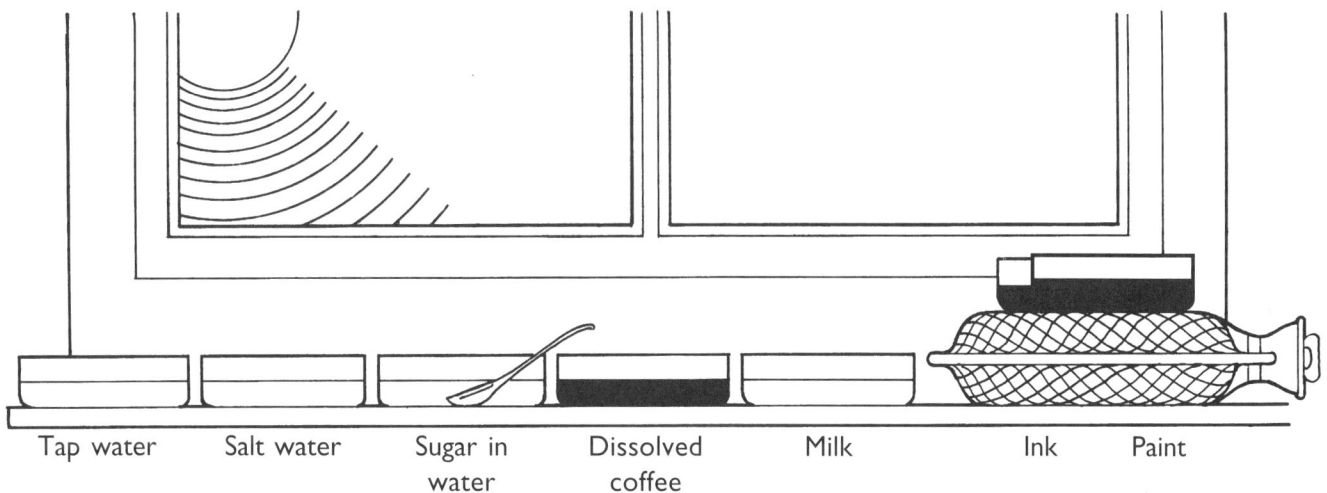

| Tap water | Salt water | Sugar in water | Dissolved coffee | Milk | Ink | Paint |

4. Draw below what you think will happen in the containers of tap water, coffee and paint when they are left to evaporate.

	After some evaporation	**After evaporation**
Tap water		
Coffee		
Paint		

Disappearing Sugar

You will need
- Dishes
- Different types of sugar (e.g. icing, caster, granulated)
- Spoon
- Stopwatch
- Water
- Measuring cyclinder
- Thermometer

Key Idea

There are different factors that affect how quickly sugar dissolves in water.

1. You are going to investigate sugar dissolving in water. Plan your investigation below. Show your plan to your teacher before you carry it out.

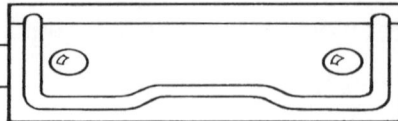

This is the question I am trying to answer:

The variable I will change is:

The variables I will keep the same are:

I will measure:

This is how I will carry out the investigation:

2. Record your results in the table below.

Type of sugar	Time for sugar to dissolve

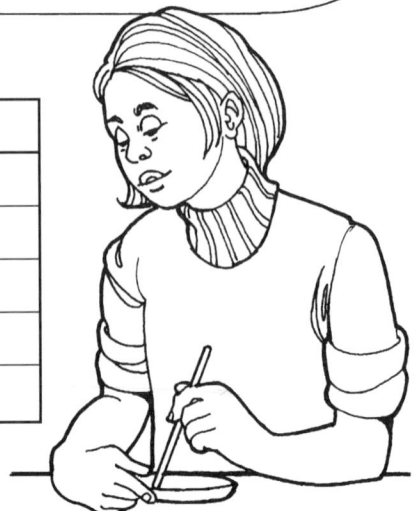

3. Plot a graph of your results.

NOW Explain what the graph tells you about dissolving sugar.

Solubility

Key Idea Different amounts of substances will dissolve in water at different temperatures.

- A group of children wanted to know how much substance would dissolve in 100ml of water. Before they investigated they each made a prediction.

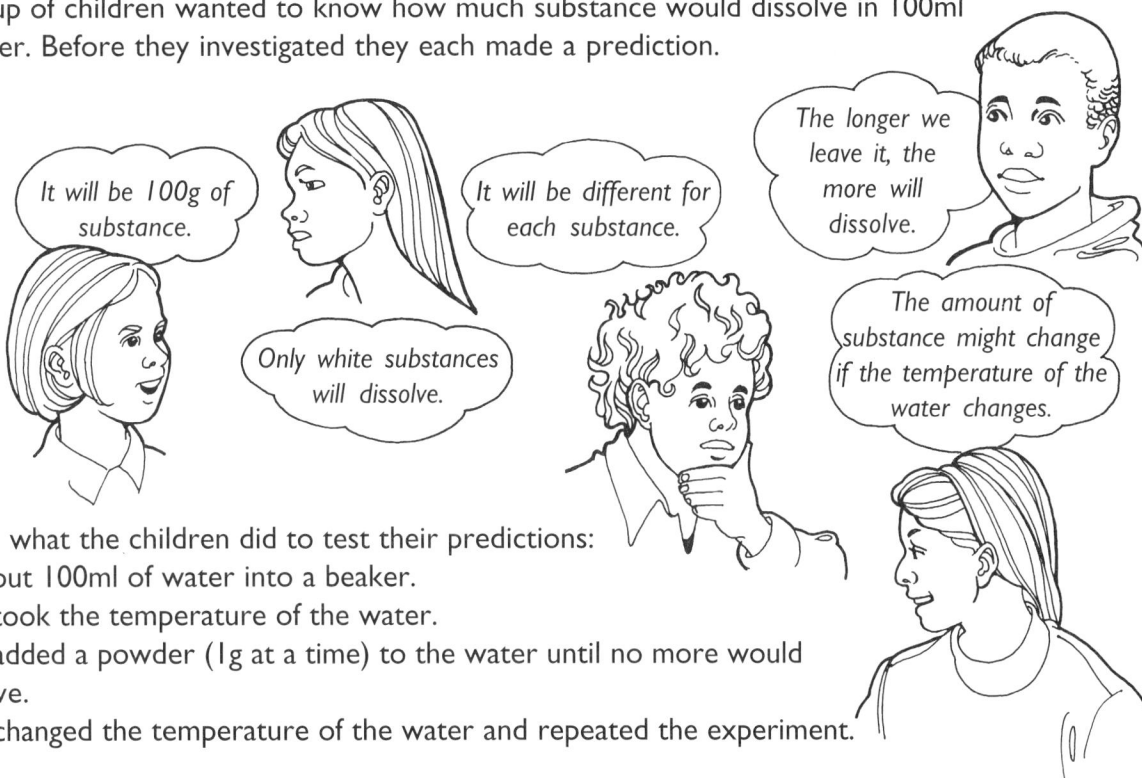

It will be 100g of substance.

Only white substances will dissolve.

It will be different for each substance.

The longer we leave it, the more will dissolve.

The amount of substance might change if the temperature of the water changes.

- This is what the children did to test their predictions:
  They put 100ml of water into a beaker.
  They took the temperature of the water.
  They added a powder (1g at a time) to the water until no more would dissolve.
  They changed the temperature of the water and repeated the experiment.

Here are the tables of their results:

White powder (1)		White powder (2)		White powder (3)		Blue powder	
Temperature	Amount dissolved	Temperature	Amount dissolved	Temperature	Amount dissolved	Temperature	Amount dissolved
20°C	11g	20°C	39g	20°C	30g	20°C	20g
40°C	14g	40°C	40g	40°C	60g	40°C	28g
60°C	17g	60°C	40g	60°C	100g	60°C	40g
80°C	20g	80°C	41g	80°C	–	80°C	60g
100°C	23g	100°C	42g	100°C	–	100°C	80g

1. Draw a graph with the axes as shown opposite. Plot the results.

2. How much of each powder do you think would have dissolved if the temperature had been 0°C?

3. Look at the predictions. Explain why each was correct or incorrect.

4. Why do you think there were no results for the white powder when the temperature was higher than 60°C?

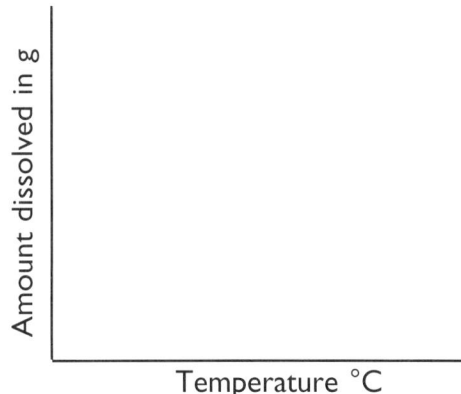

Amount dissolved in g

Temperature °C

More on Solutions

The fact that some solids dissolve in some liquids can be useful. It is one way of separating materials. Gases such as carbon dioxide can also dissolve in water although the amounts are small and difficult to measure. Children may know about this from their experience of taking the top off a fizzy-drink bottle.

Water can also dissolve pollutants. This will be dealt with later. Children should know that river water should not be drunk.

Activity pages

Washing-up Liquid
Learning objectives
- To plan how to record results.
- To present findings in an interesting way.

Give the children three different types of washing-up liquid of varying quality. Label them A, B and C and see if the children can work out which is the best and which is the worst quality. When completed tell the children the price of each brand and discuss which they think is the best value.

Cleaning Water
Learning objectives
- To observe changes taking place in the cleaning of water.
- To relate findings to industrial processes.

Water is obtained from lakes and rivers. It is screened to remove logs and fish and pumped into settlement tanks. Here the large particles fall to the bottom. The water is passed through a filter bed to remove smaller particles. Many harmful bacteria are eaten by organisms that live in the sand. Chlorine and sometimes fluorides are added to the water before it is piped to people's homes.

An alternative to this activity is given on page 50 and is intended to extend the children's investigative work.

Reclaiming the Water
Learning objectives
- To know that when a solution is boiled only the water evaporates.
- To use information to solve a problem.

When water evaporates from a solution, the solid is left behind. It is only the water that evaporates. If the evaporated water is condensed and collected in a clean container it will be pure. This process is called distillation. In some places, it is used to obtain drinking water from sea water. However, large-scale production of drinking water from sea water is a very expensive process.

Oral work

Ask the children what will happen if:
- salt solution is boiled until there is no water left
- a bowl of sugar is dropped into a cup of tea
- cocoa powder is put in cold water
- cocoa powder is put in cold milk.

Written work

Ask the children to research water treatment.

ICT

The children could use video-recording equipment to record their advert for washing-up liquid.

Washing-up Liquid

You will need
- Cooking oil
- Three different washing-up liquids
- Two medicine droppers
- Beakers
- Stirrers
- Water

Key Idea

Washing-up liquid helps grease to dissolve.

● Some children watched a television advert about washing-up liquid and asked if one brand of liquid is any better than another. You are going to carry out an investigation so that you can answer their question. Read through the instructions and plan how you are going to record your results.

1. Put 100ml water into a beaker.

 – Add five drops of cooking oil.

 – Watch what happens to the oil. How do you know the oil has not dissolved?

 – Add one drop of washing-up liquid to the water and stir.

 – Keep adding one drop and stir the water until the oil has dissolved.

 – How many drops are needed?

2. Repeat the investigation for the other washing-up liquids.

3. Write to the washing-up manufacturers explaining what you have discovered.

NOW

Make up your own television advert for the washing-up liquid that you think is the best.

Cleaning Water

Key Idea

Water from rivers and lakes is treated before it is safe to drink. Water is filtered to remove solid particles.

You will need
- Funnel filled with pebbles
- Funnel filled with grit
- Funnel filled with sand
- One litre water mixed with soil
- Beakers

● This activity will show you how dirty water can be made cleaner. Even though it may look clean it may not be safe to drink. **Do not drink it.**

1. Set up the experiment so that you have a funnel filled with pebbles, a funnel filled with grit and a funnel filled with sand.

2. Pour the dirty water through the funnel of pebbles. Look at the changes to the material in the funnel and to the water. Then pour the water through the funnel of grit and record the changes. Finally pour the resulting water through the funnel of sand.

Record your observations in the table here.

Material	Change to material	Change to water
Pebbles		
Grit		
Sand		

3. If your water is still cloudy, what could you do to make it cleaner?

4. Why is it a good idea to have different materials in the funnels to clean the water?

5. Use books to find out how water from rivers is cleaned before it is ready to drink.

6. What happens to some of the bacteria in the water?

7. What happens to some of the bacteria in the sand filter?

8. What is added to the water to make it safe?

Reclaiming the Water

You will need

- Cooker
- Pan containing salt water
- Saucer
- Two straws
- Cold pan

Key Idea

Pure water evaporates from a salt-water solution.

1. **a.** What do you think will happen when the salt water is heated to boiling point?
   b. What do you think will happen to the salt?
   c. What do you think will happen to the water?

2. Put a clean straw into the solution.
   Take it out.
   There should be a drop of liquid on the end of the straw.
   Taste the liquid.

3. Ask an adult to boil the salt water and to hold a cold pan over the steam. The pan should be tilted so that the water collects on one edge of it. The water can then be collected on a saucer.

4. Collect one drop of liquid from the saucer using another straw.
   Taste it.
   Does the liquid taste salty?

5. Were your predictions correct?

6. Explain what you think happens when salt water is heated until it boils.

7. What do you think would happen if red ink were put into a pan of water that was then heated until it boiled?

NOW

Imagine you are an engineer in a country where there is very little rain but a lot of cheap electricity. Design a machine that will use sea water to make drinking water.

Background

A reversible change involves a change of state. Examples of reversible changes are ice melting, water evaporating, salt dissolving in water, mixing salt and sand. An irreversible change involves new materials being made. Examples of irreversible changes include burning part of a candle, a nail rusting and foods being cooked or digested. The original substances cannot be obtained from the product of the change.

Activity pages

Burning Candles

Learning objectives
- To know that some changes are reversible and others irreversible.
- To observe a burning candle.

When a candle burns, the wax near the flame melts. The liquid wax is drawn up the wick. Here it becomes hotter and the wax liquid turns into wax gas. Air surrounding the wick combines with the wax gas to form carbon dioxide gas and water vapour. The black deposit left on the foil is due to incomplete burning of the carbon in the wax.

Reversible changes that the children may identify are melting/solidifying of the wax and vaporising of the liquid wax. Irreversible changes that can be identified are burning of the wax/wick.

Safety: Ensure that the children are closely supervised during this activity.

Making Gas

Learning objectives
- To plan and carry out an investigation.
- To know that carbon dioxide can be made by mixing vinegar, lemon juice or flat fizzy drink with certain substances.

When an acid is mixed with a substance that contains carbonate, carbon dioxide is produced. Powders that contain carbonate or bicarbonate are the white powders suggested. The reaction will work better (i.e. there will be more fizzing) if the powder is finer. Eggshell, washing soda and limestone also contain carbonate.

Reversible or Irreversible?

Learning objectives
- To understand that some changes are reversible and others irreversible.

Reversible/irreversible changes with suggested explanations:

Change	Reversible or irreversible	Explanation
A matchstick burning	Irreversible	New products formed
Making toast	Irreversible	New products formed
Baking a cake	Irreversible	New products formed
Drying the washing	Reversible	Can be made wet
Melting candle wax	Reversible	Liquid wax will set when cooled
Bread going mouldy	Irreversible	New products formed
Mixing oil and vinegar	Reversible	Oil and vinegar will separate out
A nail rusting	Irreversible	New products formed
A germinating seed	Irreversible	New products formed
Eating crisps	Irreversible	New products formed
Water vapour condensing on a cold window	Reversible	Water evaporates if window becomes warmer
Adding salt to water	Reversible	Salt obtained by evaporating water
Freezing water	Reversible	Water melts
Burning natural gas	Irreversible	New products formed
Stretching an elastic band	Reversible	Band contracts if force is removed
Lighting a firework	Irreversible	New products formed
Magnetising a nail	Reversible	Demagnetised by dropping
Melting fat	Reversible	Will solidify when cooled

Oral work

Ask the children to compare the burning of a candle with the burning of gas, petrol or coal. The products of burning any fossil fuel are carbon dioxide and water. Pollutants may also be made. For example, sulphur dioxide comes from the burning of coal and oil. Discuss the need for fuel, oxygen (in the air) and heat for the process of burning to take place.

Ask the children for examples of reversible and irreversible changes. Encourage them to relate everyday observations to this work.

Written work

Ask the children to construct a diagram using the following terms: 'reversible', 'irreversible', 'melting', 'freezing', 'boiling', 'condensing', 'dissolving', 'evaporating', 'heating', 'burning', 'rusting', 'baking', 'solid', 'liquid', 'gas'.

ICT

Ask the children to use a desktop-publishing program to produce a leaflet that explains reversible and irreversible changes.

Burning Candles

Key Idea Many changes occur when a candle burns.

1. In a small groups, observe a burning candle.
   Make a list of your observations. (One group of children had over 20 observations in their list.)

2. Draw your burning candle using crayons.

3. **a.** Use a peg to hold a piece of aluminium foil in the flame.
   b. What happens to the foil?

   _____

   _____

   _____

4. **a.** Use a peg to hold the burned-out match in the molten wax.
   Put it into the flame of the candle.
   b. What happens to the match?

   _____

   _____

   c. Explain why you think this happens.

   _____

   _____

5. **a.** Ask your teacher to strike a match.
   Blow out the candle.
   Your teacher should immediately move the lit match to just above the wick of the candle.
   b. What happens to the candle?

   _____

   _____

   c. Explain why you think this happens.

   _____

   _____

6. Some of the changes that take place when a candle burns are reversible.
   Name two reversible changes.

7. Some of the changes that take place are irreversible.
   Name one irreversible change.

Making Gas

Key Idea

When vinegar, lemon juice or flat fizzy drink is added to some substances there is an irreversible change. A new substance is formed.

You will need

- Test tubes or small transparent containers
- Vinegar
- Lemon juice
- Flat fizzy drink
- Stirrers
- Teaspoons
- Bicarbonate of soda
- Baking powder
- Eggshell
- Washing soda
- Small pieces of limestone and cement

- If you mix one of the liquids with one of the solids you should be able to see small bubbles of carbon dioxide gas being made.

1. **a.** Which mixture of liquid and solid will work the best? Plan an investigation to find out. You will need to define what 'best' means before you begin.

   b. Use a level teaspoon of solid and up to three teaspoons of liquid for each test.

   c. What will you do to find out which combination works best?

   d. What will you observe?

   e. How will you record your results?

2. Check your plan with your teacher before carrying out the investigation.

☞ **NOW**   Find out what the uses of carbon dioxide are.

Reversible or Irreversible?

Key Idea Some changes are reversible. Some changes are irreversible and a new material is often formed in these cases.

● Write down whether you think the following changes are reversible or irreversible. Explain your answer in each case. The first one has been done for you.

Change	Reversible or irreversible	Explanation
A matchstick burning	Irreversible	New products formed
Making toast		
Baking a cake		
Drying the washing		
Melting candle wax		
Bread going mouldy		
Mixing oil and vinegar		
A nail rusting		
A germinating seed		
Eating crisps		
Water vapour condensing on a cold window		
Adding salt to water		
Freezing water		
Burning natural gas		
Stretching an elastic band		
Lighting a firework		
Magnetising a nail		
Melting fat		

Background

A force is a push or a pull. A force can cause things to change their speed, direction or shape.

When a material is stretched the molecules in it are put under tension. As soon as the force is released the molecular forces pull the material back to its original position. A material breaks if the forces pulling the molecules apart are too large for the molecules to pull back.

Weight is a force that is commonly confused with mass. The force due to gravity is what gives us our weight. Weight changes if gravity changes. Mass is a measure of the amount of substance in an object. It stays constant throughout the Universe. In outer space our mass would be the same as it is on Earth.

A push or pull force can only act on an object if it is touching it. If we throw a ball into the air, the force of the throw is nothing once the ball is out of our hand. The ball will continue to move. If there were no other forces acting on it, the ball would carry on moving for ever. However, gravity is a force and this causes the ball to slow down and then fall back to Earth. Friction is a force. It always acts in the opposite direction to movement. Friction is useful when we are walking or applying brakes. Sometimes it is a disadvantage (e.g. when it causes wear and tear).

Activity pages

Stretching Rubber
Learning objectives
- To understand that the stretch of a rubber band depends on the force acting on it.
- To make careful measurements.
- To identify patterns in data.

The children should get a straight-line graph if they measure the extension or length of the rubber band against the force. They should be able to extrapolate the line to predict the extension if more weight were added. However, they should realise that too much force will break the rubber band.

Safety: Ensure the children have attached the rubber band firmly to a support and that they do not put their feet under the masses.

Weight
Learning objectives
- To measure using a forcemeter.
- To understand that weight is caused by gravity.

Weight is due to gravity – a force that acts towards the centre of a planet. The larger a planet, the more likely it is to have more gravity and so objects will weigh more. Saturn and Jupiter are larger than Earth, which results in objects weighing more there than here. Because the gravity is less on the Moon than on Earth objects are much lighter. It would be possible to jump higher or hit a tennis ball further on the Moon.

Where Are the Forces?
Learning objectives
- To identify the direction in which forces act.

Answers to activity sheet
a. Pull, friction
b. Pull, weight
c. Pull, weight
d. Push, friction
e. Push, weight
f. Push, weight

Oral work

Discuss other materials that are stretchy and why it might be important to know how much a material stretches. Ask the children to consider rope, steel cable, rubber tyres and skin.

Written work

Ask the children to imagine what it would be like moving about on the Moon and then on Jupiter. They could write a story or poem about how it might feel.

ICT

Using spreadsheets, ask the children to display the data from the 'Stretching Rubber' activity sheet.

Show children a video of the first landing on the Moon. A hammer and feather were dropped simultaneously. They both fell slowly giving further evidence that the gravity is less than on Earth. (The feather fell at the same rate as there was no air resistance to slow it down.)

Stretching Rubber

The amount of stretch on a rubber band depends on the force stretching it.

You will need
- Several rubber bands of different thicknesses
- 100g weights and holder
- Metre stick

1. Plan an investigation to find out what happens when weights are hung from the end of a rubber band.

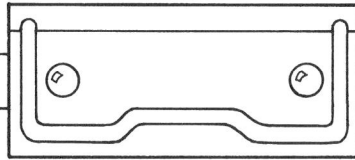

This is the question I am trying to answer:

The variables are:

I will change:

I will keep the following the same:

I will measure:

This is how I will do the investigation:

I will record my results like this:

I predict the following will happen:

2. Show your plan to your teacher before you begin the investigation.

3. Put your results into a spreadsheet and display them as a graph.

4. What do your results mean?

5. How reliable was your test and how could you have made it better?

Weight

Key Idea

Weight is caused by gravity. Gravity varies throughout the solar system, so weight varies too.

1. a. Scientists measure weight in Newtons. Predict the weight of your six objects, and enter the information into the table below.

b. Weigh your objects using the forcemeter. Record your results in the third column of the table below.

Object	Predicted weight	Weight on Earth	Weight on the Moon	Weight on Mars	Weight on Jupiter

2. Use the following information to find out how much your objects would weigh if you took them to the Moon, Mars and Jupiter. Record your results in the table.

- The gravity on the Earth causes things to weigh about six times more than they do on the Moon.
- The gravity on Mars causes objects to weigh about one third of what they weigh on Earth.
- The gravity on Jupiter causes objects to weigh about 2.5 times what they weigh on Earth.

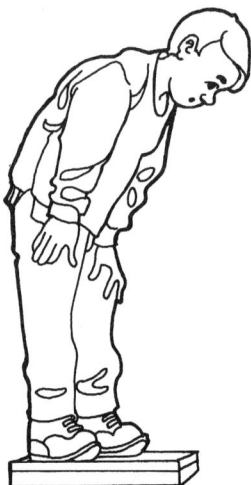

3. Why do you think objects weigh the most on Jupiter?

4. Why do you think objects weigh the least on the Moon?

5. How could you find out how much you would weigh on Jupiter?

NOW

Find information about other planets. On which planets do you think we would weigh more than we do on Earth? Explain your answer.

Where Are the Forces?

 **Key Idea**

Forces act in a particular direction.

1. Look at the pictures below.
   Decide whether the person is using a push or a pull on the object.

2. Decide what force the person is trying to overcome.

3. Draw two arrows where the forces are acting on the object. The arrows will need to touch the object. If the force is large then draw a larger arrow than for a small force.

a.

d.

b.

e.

c.

f.

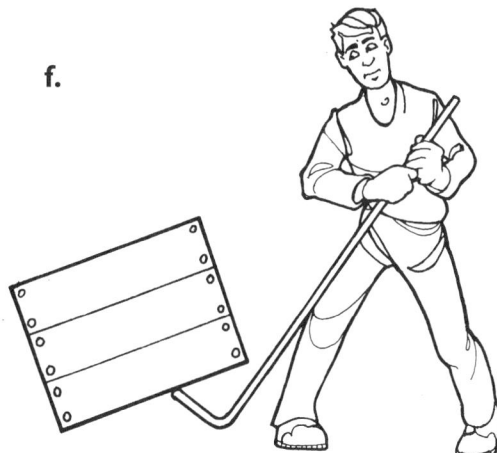

BELAIR ACTIVE SCIENCE 6

Floating and Sinking

Background

When an object is placed in water some of the water is displaced and causes the object to weigh less in water. The water that is displaced produces an upward force on the object equal to the weight of the water. This upward force is called upthrust. If the upthrust is equal to the weight of the object in air then the object floats. The forces are said to be balanced.

Activity pages

Changing Weight

Learning objectives
- To understand that objects appear to 'weigh' less when placed in water.
- To understand that objects that float appear to be 'weightless'.

Examples of heavy objects that float are: candle wax, plastic bottles with sand in, margarine cartons containing grit. The children should notice that objects appear to 'weigh' less when placed in water. They should also realise that when objects float they appear to 'weigh' nothing.

You could make an object such as a bottle of lemonade float by taking out some of the lemonade, putting it on something that floats (e.g. swimming floats, toy boat) or attaching balloons around its middle.

Making a Cartesian Diver

Learning objectives
- To know that changing the weight of a Cartesian diver causes it to float or sink.

When the bottle is squeezed, the increased air pressure forces water into the stem of the dropper. This causes the dropper to become heavier and so it sinks. When the pressure on the bottle is removed, some of the water leaves the stem of the dropper; it becomes lighter and floats.

The Plimsoll Line
- To understand that floating objects displace their own weight of water.
- To know that the Plimsoll Line was developed to make ships safer.

Objects float in a liquid if their density is less than that of the liquid. Density can be calculated as mass divided by volume. The density of water changes as the temperature changes. When heated, water expands; its volume becomes bigger. For example, $1\,cm^3$ of hot water weighs less than $1\,cm^3$ of cold water. $1\,cm^3$ sea water weighs more than $1\,cm^3$ fresh water – salt water has a greater density than fresh water. It is for this reason that Plimsoll need to develop a set of lines that would make shipping safer throughout the world.

Answers to Plimsoll Line

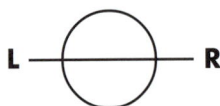

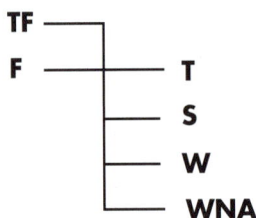

Oral work

Plimsoll was a Member of Parliament in the 1850s. The children could listen to a recent debate in the House of Commons and develop their own speech either for or against the introduction of the Plimsoll Line.

Written work

Ask the children to write an explanation of why some light things sink and some heavy things float (e.g. why does a paper clip sink but an iron boat float or why does an unpeeled grapefruit float but a peeled grapefruit sink?).

ICT

Ask the children to use a word-processing program to write a newspaper article describing the circumstances that led to the sinking of a ship laden with cargo.

Changing 'Weight'

You will need
- Forcemeter
- Eight objects (some of which float and some of which sink)
- Bowl of water
- Rubber bands

Key Idea

When objects are placed in water their 'weight' appears to change due to upthrust.

● You are going to investigate what happens to the 'weight' of an object when it is placed in water.

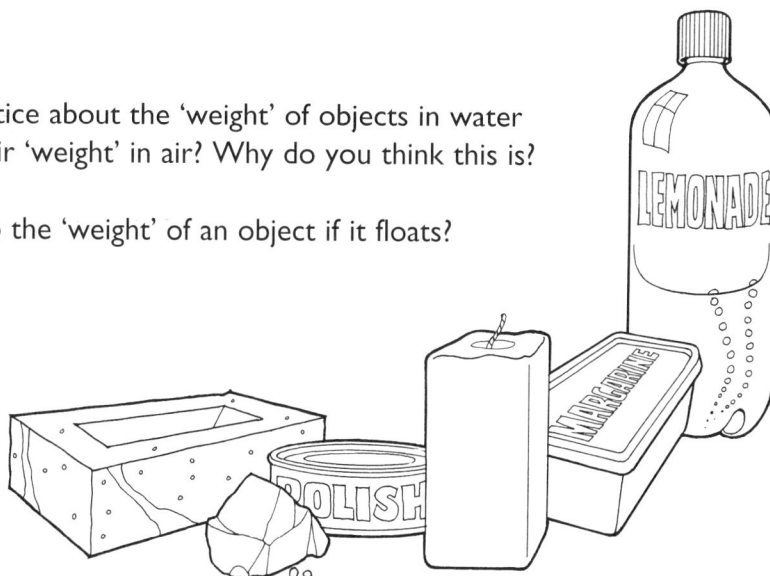

1. The investigation works better if you use heavy objects. Why do you think that might be?

2. Carry out your investigation and record your results in the table below. To 'weigh' the objects, fasten rubber bands around them and hang the bands from a forcemeter. Make sure that the bands will not slip off.

Object	'Weight' in air	'Weight' in water

3. What do you notice about the 'weight' of objects in water compared to their 'weight' in air? Why do you think this is?

4. What happens to the 'weight' of an object if it floats?

NOW

Think of two different ways you could make one of the objects that sank in your experiment float.

Making a Cartesian Diver

You will need
- Screw-top plastic bottle
- Water
- Medicine dropper
- Plasticine
- Beaker

Key Idea — Changing the amount of liquid in a Cartesian diver causes it to float or sink.

1. Make a Cartesian diver by following the instructions below.

- Put the medicine dropper vertically into a beaker of water. You should see that it floats with a lot of the rubber above the waterline.

- Add plasticine to the bottom of the dropper until it just floats in the water.

- Now, put water into the plastic bottle until it is 1cm from the top.

- Put the medicine dropper vertically into the bottle.

- Screw on the top.

- Gently squeeze the bottle and observe what happens.

LID
MOST OF THE RUBBER ABOVE SURFACE
PLASTICINE
DROPPER
WATER
PLASTIC BOTTLE

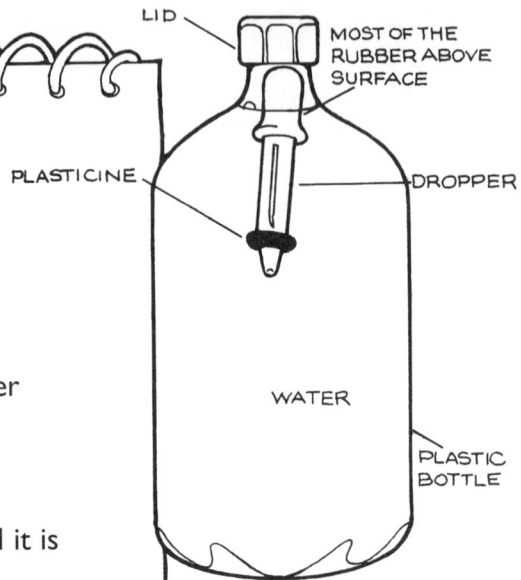

2. What happens to the diver when you squeeze the bottle?

3. What happens to the diver when you stop squeezing?

4. What happens to the level of water in the dropper when the bottle is squeezed?

5. What happens to the level cof water in the dropper when you stop squeezing?

6. Explain how you think the diver works.

BELAIR ACTIVE SCIENCE 6

The Plimsoll Line

A floating object displaces its own weight of water. There is a safe limit for the load that a ship can carry.

1. Read the following.

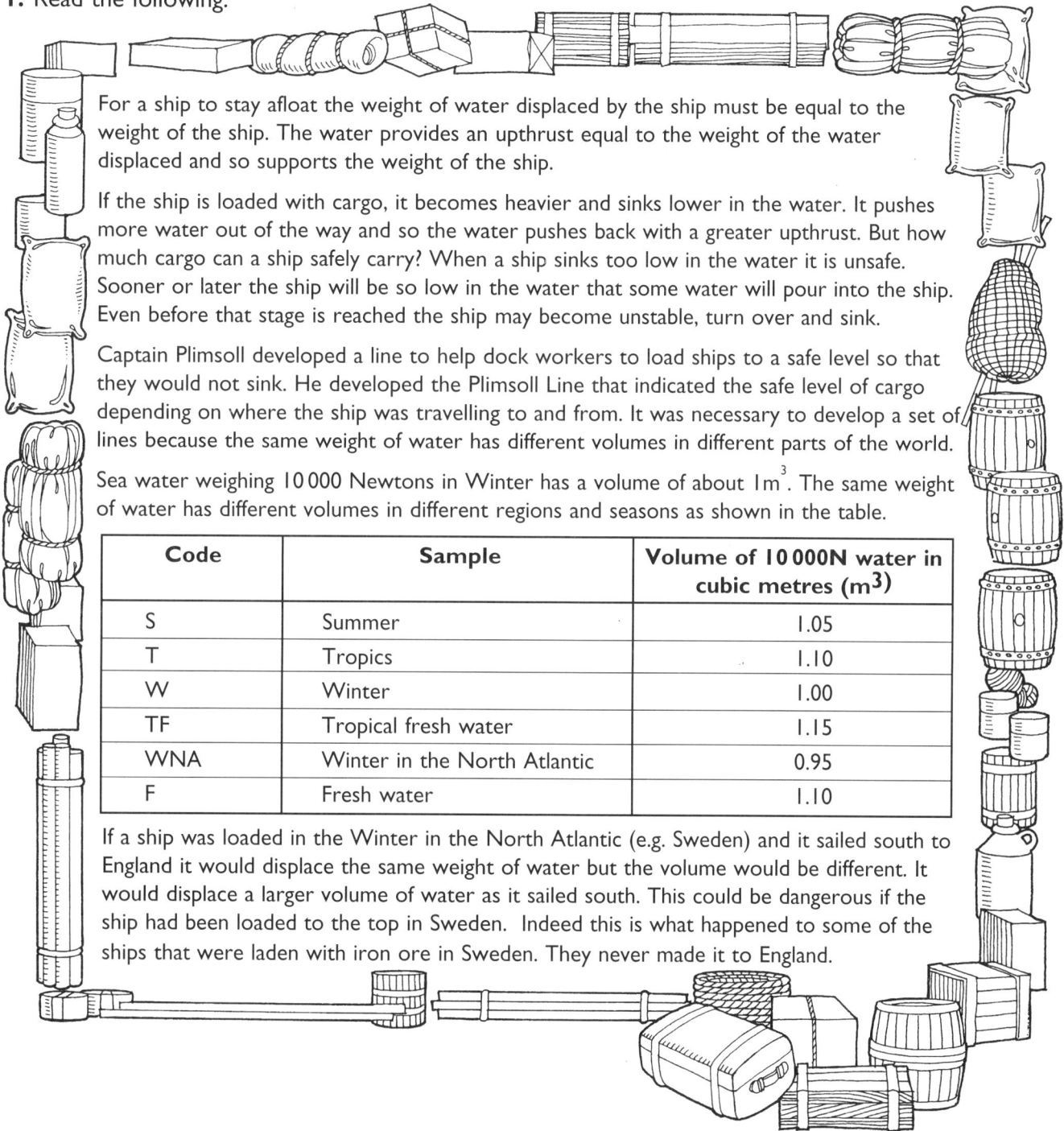

For a ship to stay afloat the weight of water displaced by the ship must be equal to the weight of the ship. The water provides an upthrust equal to the weight of the water displaced and so supports the weight of the ship.

If the ship is loaded with cargo, it becomes heavier and sinks lower in the water. It pushes more water out of the way and so the water pushes back with a greater upthrust. But how much cargo can a ship safely carry? When a ship sinks too low in the water it is unsafe. Sooner or later the ship will be so low in the water that some water will pour into the ship. Even before that stage is reached the ship may become unstable, turn over and sink.

Captain Plimsoll developed a line to help dock workers to load ships to a safe level so that they would not sink. He developed the Plimsoll Line that indicated the safe level of cargo depending on where the ship was travelling to and from. It was necessary to develop a set of lines because the same weight of water has different volumes in different parts of the world.

Sea water weighing 10 000 Newtons in Winter has a volume of about $1m^3$. The same weight of water has different volumes in different regions and seasons as shown in the table.

Code	Sample	Volume of 10 000N water in cubic metres (m^3)
S	Summer	1.05
T	Tropics	1.10
W	Winter	1.00
TF	Tropical fresh water	1.15
WNA	Winter in the North Atlantic	0.95
F	Fresh water	1.10

If a ship was loaded in the Winter in the North Atlantic (e.g. Sweden) and it sailed south to England it would displace the same weight of water but the volume would be different. It would displace a larger volume of water as it sailed south. This could be dangerous if the ship had been loaded to the top in Sweden. Indeed this is what happened to some of the ships that were laden with iron ore in Sweden. They never made it to England.

2. Here is the Plimsoll Line with some of the codes missing. Write in the codes in the correct places.

3. LR means Lloyd's Register of Shipping. Lloyd's had to pay the ship owners for their lost cargo and ships. Why do you think Lloyd's wanted Plimsoll to develop the line?

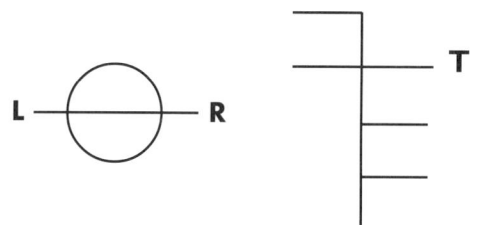

Air and Water Resistance

Background

Air resistance slows down moving objects. When objects move through the air the air gets in the way and provides a resistive force. This resistance always acts in the opposite direction to motion and so slows the object. The faster an object is moving through the air, the greater the resistance. Sports technology has developed specialist materials that reduce air resistance.

When boats move through water some of the energy is used to cause the water to move. This movement causes turbulence. The more energy wasted in producing turbulence, the less there will be to make the boat move; the boat will therefore move more slowly.

Activity pages

Paper Aeroplanes
Learning objectives
- To plan and carry out an investigation.

The children could change the shape of the wings or nose by folding or tearing them. They could also add paper clips to the wings or nose.

Moving Through Water
Learning objectives
- To observe how a change in the shape of a boat affects the way it moves through the water.

Designing and making the boats could be carried out as part of a Design and Technology activity. They need to be similar in size (e.g. 15 x 6 x 2.5cm). If balsa wood is available, children could make the boats from wood. Before testing, ask the children to predict which will be the best boat. After testing, ask them to explain why the boats travel at different speeds and why the turbulence is different for different-shaped boats.

Streamlined
Learning objectives
- To understand that the shape of objects affects their resistance.

The pictures on the left side of this sheet are all of things that benefit from air resistance. The pictures on the right are all of things that benefit from the prevention of air resistance. Other objects that benefit from air resistance include kites, gliders and yachts. Other objects that benefit from the prevention of air resistance include runners, racing cars and darts.

Runners will need clothes that reduce air resistance whilst allowing air to circulate around the body. Long hair needs to be tied back. Cyclists wear tight-fitting shorts and tops. Their helmets are also streamlined. The footwear is smooth and may not have laces as laces increase air resistance. Swimmers sometimes shave their head and body. They often wear tight-fitting smooth caps on their heads. They may grease their body so that the water does not attach to them.

Oral work

Link this work to the way the children dress for sports activities. Ask them why it is important to close their tracksuit top when they are playing football or running. Ask them to consider which sports need little air resistance and which use air resistance (e.g. badminton, yachting, kite-flying). Discuss how animals have adapted to reduce air resistance.

Written work

Ask them to use the results of the activity sheet 'Moving Through Water' to prepare an advert to sell their fastest boat.

ICT

The data from activity sheet 'Moving Through Water' can be displayed using spreadsheets.

Paper Aeroplanes

You will need
- Paper
- Paper clips
- Stopwatch
- Scissors
- Tape measure

Key Idea   Air resistance slows moving objects.

1. Make a paper aeroplane and observe it as it flies.

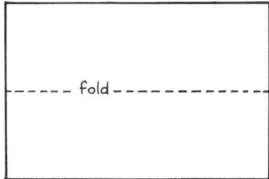

- - - fold - - - - - - -

1   Make a fold down the middle.

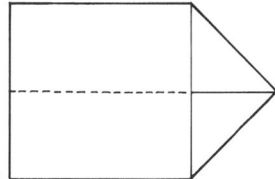

2   Fold in the corners at one end.

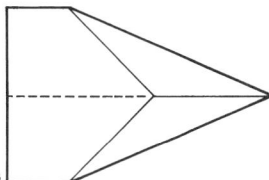

3   Fold the sides down again.

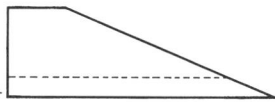

4   Fold in the middle.

2. Make a list of three questions that you could answer by carrying out an investigation using paper aeroplanes.

3. Choose one of your questions to investigate.

4. Plan your investigation below.

keel

nose

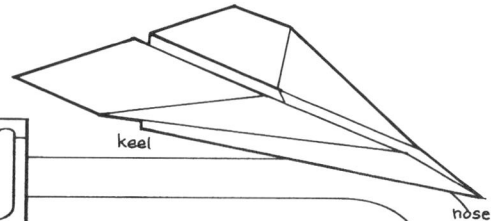

Here is my question:

I will change:

I will measure:

I will keep the following the same:

This is how I will do the investigation:

I will record my results like this:

I predict the following will happen:

5. Show your plan to your teacher before you begin the investigation.

6. What do your results mean?

7. How reliable was your test and how could you have made it better?

Moving Through Water

The shape of an object affects the way it moves through the water.

1. Set up the test tank as shown below.

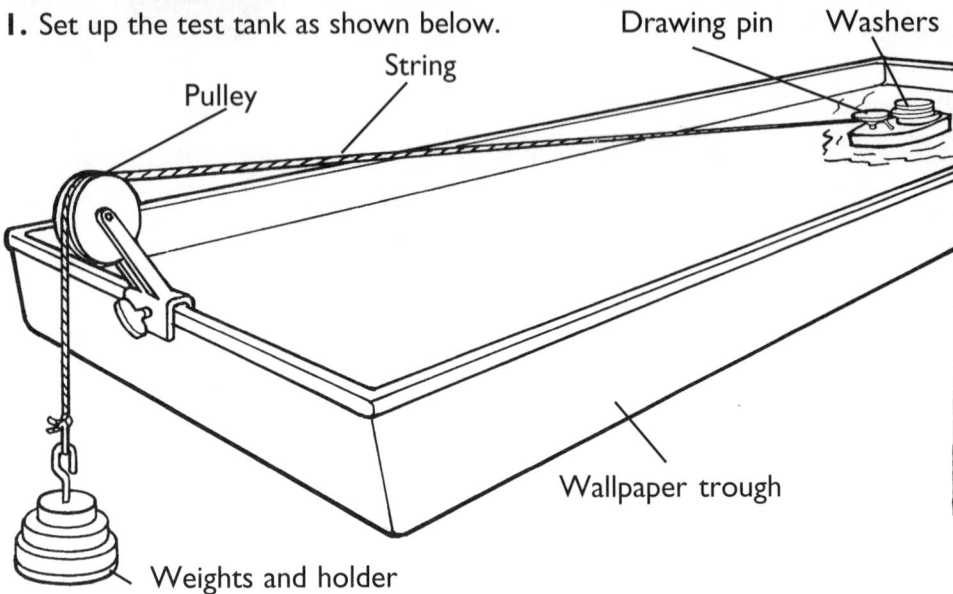

Pulley

String

Drawing pin   Washers

Wallpaper trough

Weights and holder

2. Attach the string to one end of the boat.
Add washers to the boat so that it is in the water to a depth of about 1cm.
Place just enough weight on the holder for the boat to move smoothly through the water.
Be careful not to add too much.
Observe the turbulence as the boat moves through the water. Record the wave patterns.

3. Measure the time it takes for the boat to travel to the end of the tank.
Repeat your measurements four more times and calculate the average.

4. Now repeat the experiment with each of your other boats.

5. Record your results in a graph.

6. What is the pattern between the time it took for the boat to travel and the amount of turbulence?

NOW

If you were a boat builder which of the boats would you be most likely to build? Explain your answer.

Streamlined

1. The pictures below have been sorted into two groups. How do you think they have been sorted?

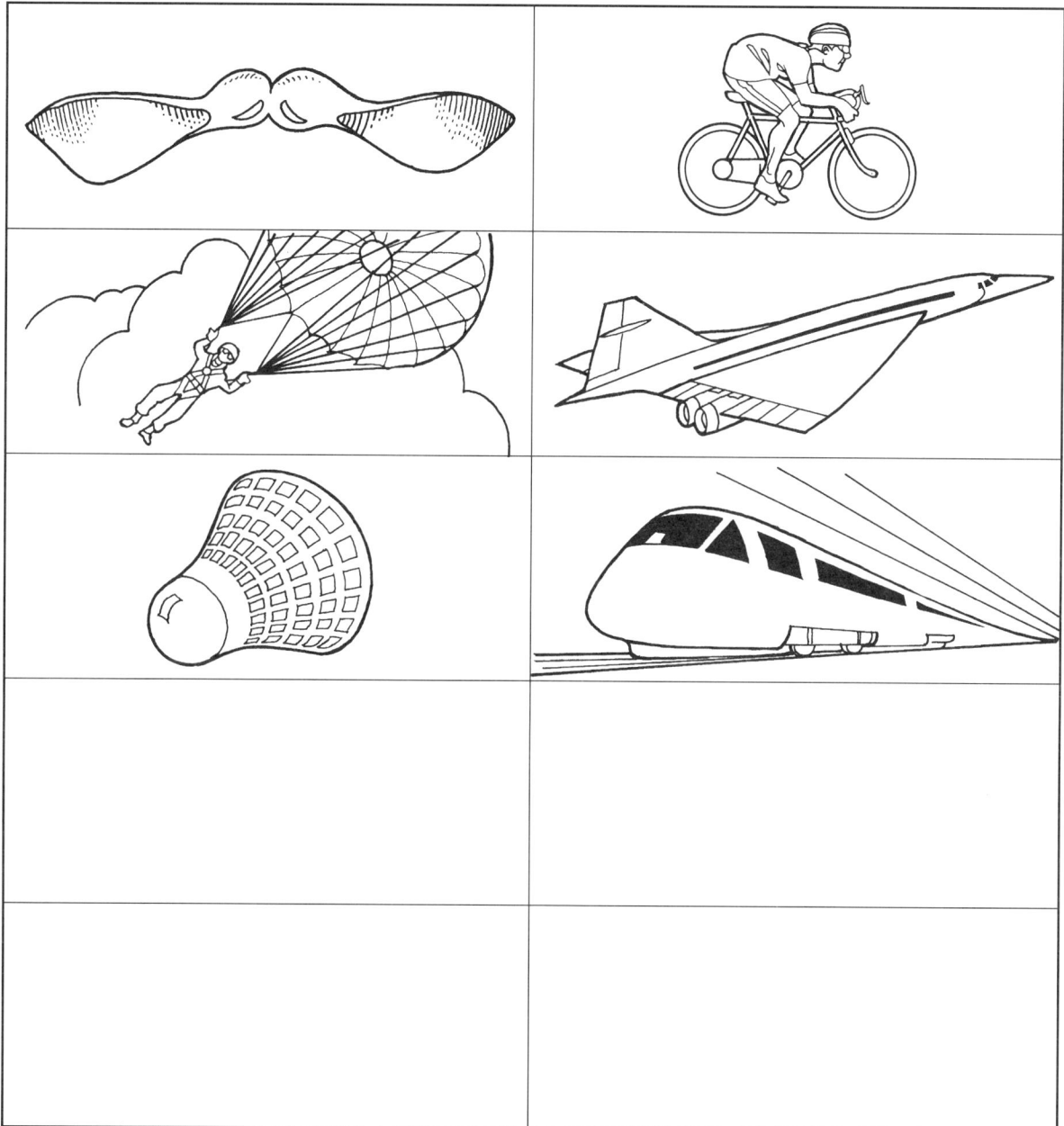

2. To each group, add pictures of two other examples.

3. Explain how each object is suited to its group.

NOW

The triathlon consists of three events: running, swimming and cycling. Imagine your friends are going to enter a triathlon competition. Write a letter to them telling them what they need to do in order to race as fast as possible.

Images and Shadows

Background

Light can be reflected from shiny surfaces. The direction of the reflection can be changed by changing the angle of the surface. The rays that strike a surface are called the incident rays and those that leave a surface are called the reflected rays. The angle between the incident rays and a line drawn at right angles to the mirror is the same as that for the reflected rays. The image in a plane mirror is the same size as the object; it is the same way up but it is laterally inverted. This means that the right-hand side of the object becomes the left-hand side of the image.

Shadows are formed when the path of light is blocked. The size of a shadow can be affected by the object's size, the distance from the light source, the size of the light source and the distance of the object from the screen.

Activity pages

Angles of Reflection
Learning objectives
- To find a relationship between the direction of light striking a mirror and the reflected light.

The light striking a mirror is known as the incident ray. The investigation can also be carried out on a sunny day using a comb standing on a white piece of paper. If the mirror is placed diagonally across the shadows, the paths of the incident and reflected light can be compared.

The children should find that the angle between the incident ray and the mirror and between the reflected light and the mirror are similar.

What Makes a Mirror?
Learning objectives
- To know that shiny surfaces reflect light better than dull surfaces.
- To draw conclusions from comparisons.

Good reflective surfaces reflect light so that a detailed image is formed. On poorer reflective surfaces some light is absorbed, some light is scattered and only some of the reflected light enters our eyes.

Safety – The children should be warned about the dangers of reflecting sunlight into their own or into others' eyes.

Changing Shadow Size
Learning objectives
- To display results in a graphical form.
- To interpret results.

The further from the torch, the shorter the shadow size of the stick.

As the torch is moved further from the stick, less light is blocked out and so the shadow becomes shorter. The minimum length of the shadow will be the length of the stick. If the stick were moved away from the screen the size of the shadow would increase.

The 30cm result needs to be checked as it gives an anomalous result.

Oral work

Encourage the children to use words accurately. 'Reflection' is the process of reflecting. An 'image' is what you see in a mirror. A 'reversed image' will be observed if children look at themselves in a mirror.

Discuss some common examples of reflective surfaces and the use of mirrors. Discuss why we can see ourselves in still water but not when it is rippled. Why can we not see ourselves in a steamed-up mirror?

Written work

Ask the children to explain how and where mirrors are used.

They could also research the different types of mirrors.

ICT

Use a drawing package (e.g. Kaleidoscope) to create symmetrical patterns similar to those seen in a mirror.

Angles of Reflection

You will need

- Darkened room
- Plastic mirror
- Plasticine
- Sheet of paper
- Torch covered with black card with a slit down the middle
- Angle indicator

Key Idea

Mirrors can be used to change the direction of light.

1. Stand the mirror vertically on a sheet of paper and support it with plasticine in front and books behind. Draw a line on the paper along the edge of the mirror.

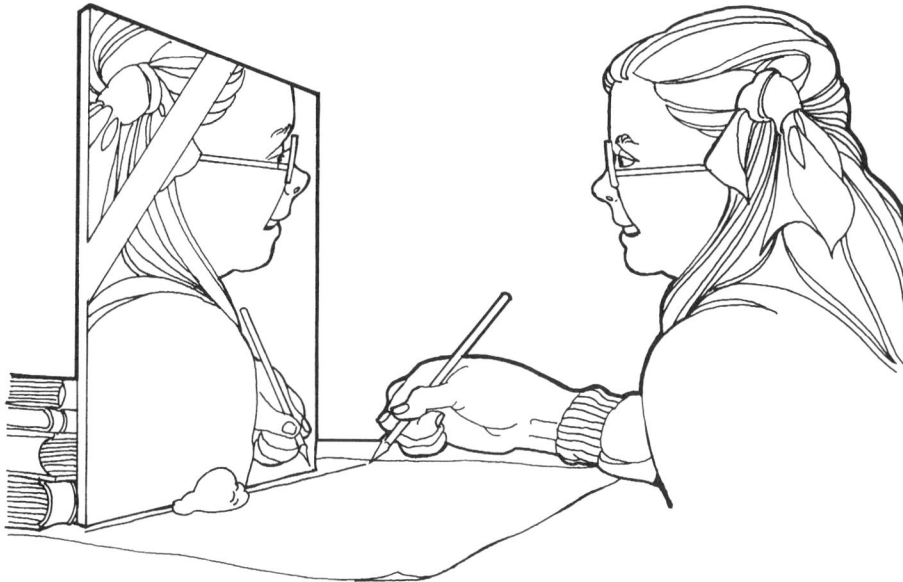

2. In a darkened room, hold a piece of black card with a slit down the middle in front of a torch. Shine a beam of light from a torch along the sheet of paper and on to the mirror.

3. Draw a line on the paper to show where the beam comes from.

4. Draw another line to show where the beam is reflected. Label your lines.

5. Reposition the torch and repeat the experiment three times.

6. **a.** For each beam, measure the angle between the incoming beam and the mirror.
   b. Measure the angle between the reflected beam and the mirror.
   c. Record your results in a table. What pattern do you notice?

7. Use two mirrors to see the back of your head. Draw a picture to show how you did this.

What Makes a Mirror?

Key Idea

Shiny surfaces reflect better than dull surfaces.

You will need

- Mirror
- Perspex
- Polished metals
- Aluminium foil
- Polished and unpolished wood
- Shiny and matt paper
- Shiny and matt painted surfaces
- Large bowl of water
- Piece of rubber

1. Look at each of the surfaces and put them in order according to how well they reflect light. Order them, in the box below, from the most to the least reflective.

Surfaces

2. How did you decide whether one surface was better at reflecting light than another?

3. What type of surfaces make the best reflectors?

4. Explain what you think happens to light when it strikes a good reflector. Draw a diagram to help.

NOW

Explain what you think happens to light when it strikes a poor reflective surface. Draw a diagram to help.

Changing Shadow Size

Shadow size changes as the distance from the light source changes. Graphs can help to identify incorrect results.

● A group of children carried out an experiment to find out what happens to the size of a stick's shadow as they move the light source further from the stick. Here is a table of their results.

Distance of torch from object	Length of the shadow
10cm	14.2cm
20cm	10.7cm
30cm	10.1cm
40cm	7.9cm
50cm	7.4cm
60cm	6.8cm
70cm	6.4cm

1. Draw a graph of the children's results.

2. What is the pattern?

3. Which of the readings do you think the children should do again?

4. Draw a diagram to help to explain what the children's results mean.

5. What do you think the length of the shadow would be if the torch were placed 5cm away from the stick?

6. What do you think the length of the shadow would be if the torch were placed 80cm away from the stick?

7. What do you think would happen to the size of the shadow if the stick were moved away from the screen?

Background

The activities should be used to help to consolidate the children's previous learning and to encourage them to apply their understanding to problem-solving situations. Electric current is the flow of charge around a circuit. It can only flow when a circuit is complete. The electricity is pumped from the battery through the circuit and back to the battery. Electrical energy can be converted into light, heat or movement.

Activity pages

Changing Wires

Learning objectives
- To ask questions that can be answered by investigation.
- To know that the length or thickness of a wire affects bulb brightness.

The children will need to use thin fuse wire in this investigation. They may need to modify their original plan to obtain any useful results (e.g. they will need to compare lengths of wire). To increase the thickness of the wire they could use two, three, four or five pieces wound together.

The children should find out that the longer the wire, the dimmer the bulb will be (there is more resistance). The thinner wire will also make a dimmer bulb (again there is more resistance). Adding more pieces in parallel will reduce the resistance, enabling the bulb to glow more brightly.

Changing Speed

Learning objectives
- To apply knowledge to solve a problem.
- To know how to change the speed of a motor.

Reducing the flow of the current will reduce the speed of the motor. This can be achieved by lowering the voltage of the electricity supply in the circuit or by increasing the resistance of the circuit as a whole (e.g. adding bulbs, lengths of fuse wire).

Circuit Diagrams

Learning objectives
- To know conventional symbols for components in circuits.
- To interpret circuit diagrams.

Answers to the activity sheet
2 The bulb will not light as the switch is open. The circuit is not complete.
3 The motor will turn and the bulb will light as the circuit is complete. Children may recognise that they need a large battery if both components are to work.
4 The buzzer will not work as there is no power supply to the circuit.
5 The bulbs will not light as there is a break in the circuit.
6 The bulbs will not light as the switch is open.
7 The motor and the bulb will work as the circuit is complete.

Oral work

Discuss with the children other occasions when it may be necessary to reduce the current in a circuit (e.g. dimmer switches, volume control).

Written work

Ask the children to imagine that they are part of an electric current and to write a story or poem describing their journey through a circuit. At the start of their journey they will have lots of energy but by the time they return they will have none left. Most of their energy will have converted to heat.

ICT

Ask the children to research how electrical components (e.g. bulb, switch, buzzer) work and then to make a model using thin card to help them to explain this to others.

Changing Wires

Key Idea

The length and thickness of a wire affect the brightness of a bulb.

You will need

- Different thicknesses and lengths of fuse wire
- Battery and battery holder
- Bulb and bulb holder
- Leads

1. What difference will different lengths or thicknesses of wire have on the brightness of a bulb? Plan an investigation to find out.

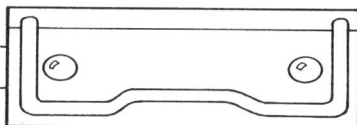

I will change:

I will keep the following the same:

I will measure:

This is how I will do the investigation:

This is how I will set up the circuit:

Circuit diagram

I predict the following will happen:

2. Carry out the investigation.

3. Complete the following sentence:

When I increased the _____ of the wire, the bulb glowed _____ brightly.

4. Draw a diagram to help you to explain what might be happening inside the wire.

Changing Speed

Key Idea

The speed of a motor can be changed.

You will need
- White card
- Pens
- Battery
- Motor
- Rotor blades
- Leads
- Resistant material to reduce flow of electricity (e.g. bulbs, fuse wire)

● Nita and Ali supported different sports teams. They each had a magic badge. When their team was winning, the badge spun and the more they were winning, the faster it went. Sometimes the teams lost their games. It was at times like these that the badges did not spin at all.

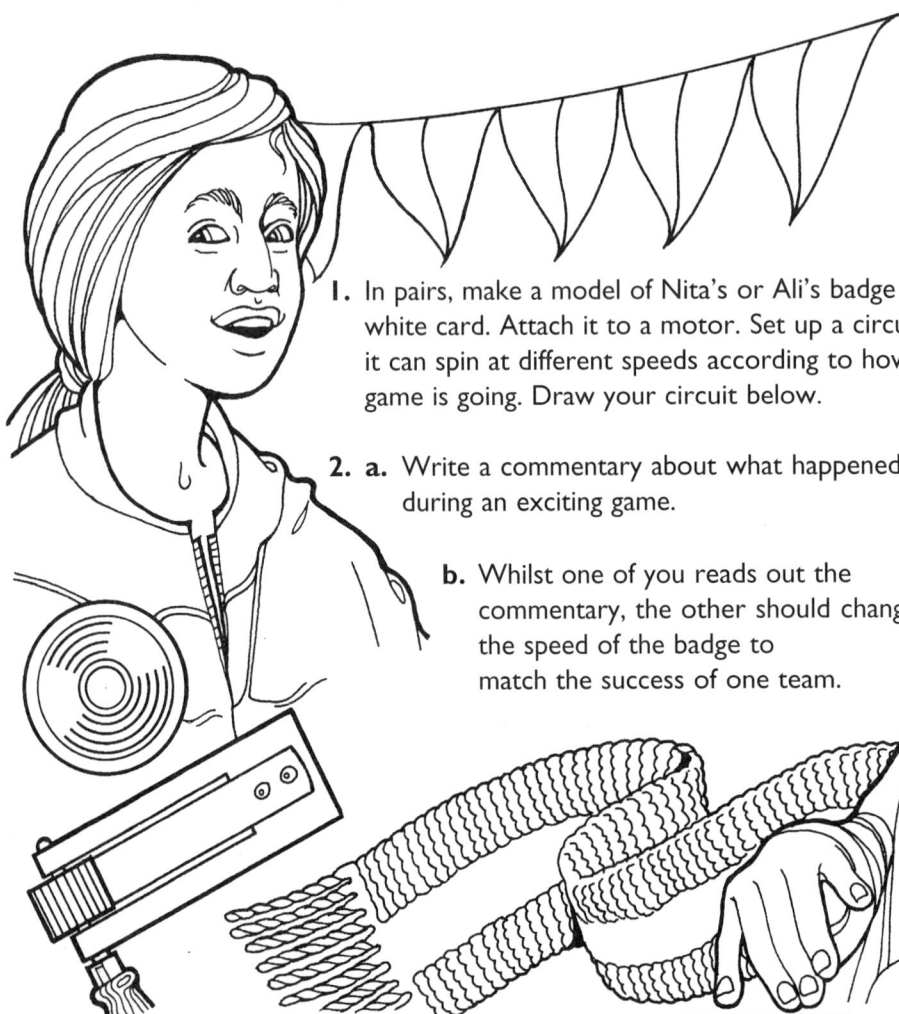

1. In pairs, make a model of Nita's or Ali's badge from white card. Attach it to a motor. Set up a circuit so that it can spin at different speeds according to how well the game is going. Draw your circuit below.

2. **a.** Write a commentary about what happened during an exciting game.

   b. Whilst one of you reads out the commentary, the other should change the speed of the badge to match the success of one team.

My circuit

Circuit Diagrams

Key Idea	Symbols can be used to represent electrical circuits.

Circuit symbols

Cell: | | Buzzer: (B)   Switch (open): —✓•—   Switch (closed): —•—•—   Bulb: ⊗   Motor: (M)

- The diagrams above show how components are represented in electrical circuits. Below are some circuit diagrams. For each diagram explain what will happen and why. The first one has been done for you.

	Circuit diagram	Explanation of what will happen
1		The bulbs will light because there is a complete circuit. The switch is closed so the electricity will flow from the battery to the bulbs and back to the battery.
2		
3		
4		
5		
6		
7		

The unit will enable pupils to develop their investigative skills in an environmental or technological context. The environmental investigation relates to 'adaptation'. The investigation relating to the cleaning of water will help pupils to develop skills in both environmental and technological contexts. The final page of this chapter provides the children with some prompt questions for carrying out further investigations of their own. Other activities throughout the book encourage pupils to develop their scientific enquiry skills and attitudes.

Activity pages

Studying Hedges and Walls
Learning objectives
- To compare animal and plant life.
- To collect and record data.
- To interpret findings.

There should be different conditions on either side of the hedge or wall (e.g. sunny/shaded, sheltered/windy). You will need to make a preliminary visit to the area so that you will be able to help the children to identify some of the plant and animal life. The children could measure from the hedge or wall and record the plants/animals found at each 50cm interval. A class survey could be collated so that a more reliable set of data is obtained. A similar activity could be carried out in two different environments (e.g. woodland and urban area).

Safety: Ensure that any off-site visits are carried out in accordance with LEA guidelines.

How Can We Clean Water?
- To plan and carry out an experiment.
- To relate findings to industrial processes.
- To extend children's investigative work in a technological context.

Water is obtained from lakes and rivers. It is screened to remove logs and fish and pumped into settlement tanks. Here the large particles fall to the bottom. The water is passed through a filter bed to remove smaller particles. Many harmful bacteria are eaten by organisms that live in the sand. Chlorine and sometimes fluorides are added to the water before it is piped to people's homes. Domestic sewage is treated in a similar way to drinking water. Only when it meets national quality standards can it be pumped into rivers and the sea.

The sheet on page 22 could be used if preferred.

My Investigation
This sheet can be used to remind children of the questions they need to consider when planning and carrying out their own investigation.

Oral work

Ask the children to discuss the positive and negative effects of scientific developments on the environment.

Topics that could be discussed are the effect of sewage farms on the environment and whether fluoride should be added to drinking water. The quality of drinking water in the 1800s can be compared to that of today.

Written work

The children could communicate their findings through posters and explanations of why certain animal or plant life is adapted to certain environments.

ICT

Data collected during the 'Studying Hedges and Walls' activity could be put into a spreadsheet and displayed graphically.

Studying Hedges and Walls

You will need
- Hedge or wall that runs east to west
- Hand lens
- Animal (insect) and plant identification books

Key Idea

Different conditions on either side of a hedge or wall will affect animal and plant life.

1. Compare the animal and plant life on either side of a hedge or wall.

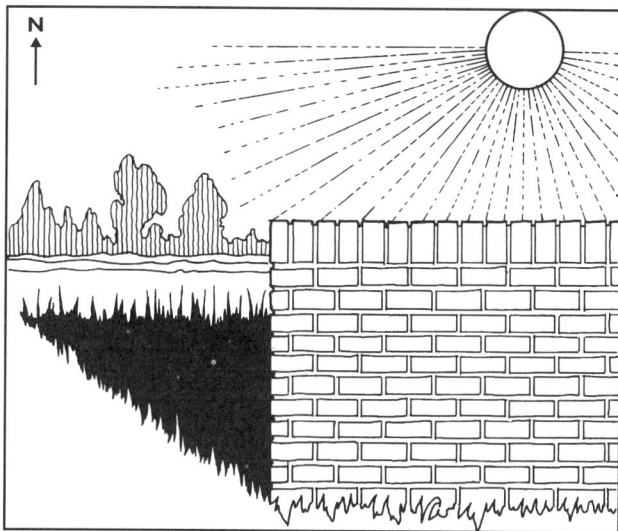

2. Why might the animal and plant life be different on either side?

3. Why might the animal and plant life be the same on either side?

4. What animals and plants might you expect to see nearby?

5. Make a list of questions you could answer by visiting the hedge or wall. For example:

- Is one side sunnier than the other?
- Is one side sheltered from the wind more than the other?
- Which plants grow only on one side?
- Which animals are found more often on one side?

6. In groups of four, decide how you will compare the life on either side of the hedge or wall.

7. How will you record your observations?

After the visit

8. What differences to animal and plant life are there between one side and the other?
Explain why these differences might be.

9. Do you think you would get the same results for all hedges or walls? Explain your reasoning.

10. If you were to revisit the site, what further investigation could you carry out to check your ideas?

How Can We Clean Water?

You will need
- Large funnels
- 200ml water mixed with soil
- Beakers
- Pebbles
- Grit
- Sand
- Piece of nylon tights or fine curtain netting
- Filter paper

Key Idea

Water from rivers and lakes is treated before it is safe to drink. Water is filtered to remove solid particles.

1. Find out which combination of three filters is the best for getting clear water from 200ml of the soil and water mixture.
Plan how you will find out which three filters to use and in which order they should be used. You will need to think about the following.

   - What observations will you record?
   - How will you record your observations?
   - What measurements will you make?
   - How will you ensure your tests are fair?
   - What will you do with the dirty filters (do not wash them in the sink)?

2. Show your planning to your teacher before you begin the investigation.

3. Make a poster to show the best way of making clear water. You will need to include:

   - an explanation of what happens to the dirty water and the filter at each stage of the process
   - an explanation of why three different filters are better than one filter
   - how much clear water you can obtain from 200ml dirty water
   - how clear your water is compared to tap water.

4. a. Imagine you are to clean very large amounts of water using three filters. How would you change your process of cleaning water?
   b. Where would you obtain your filters?
   c. What would you do with the dirty filters so that you would not pollute the environment?

NOW

Research what happens to domestic sewage to make it safe enough to be put back into the rivers or the sea. How is your method of cleaning water similar to a sewage works and how is it different?

My Investigation

Carrying out an investigation consists of three stages: planning, obtaining evidence and considering evidence.

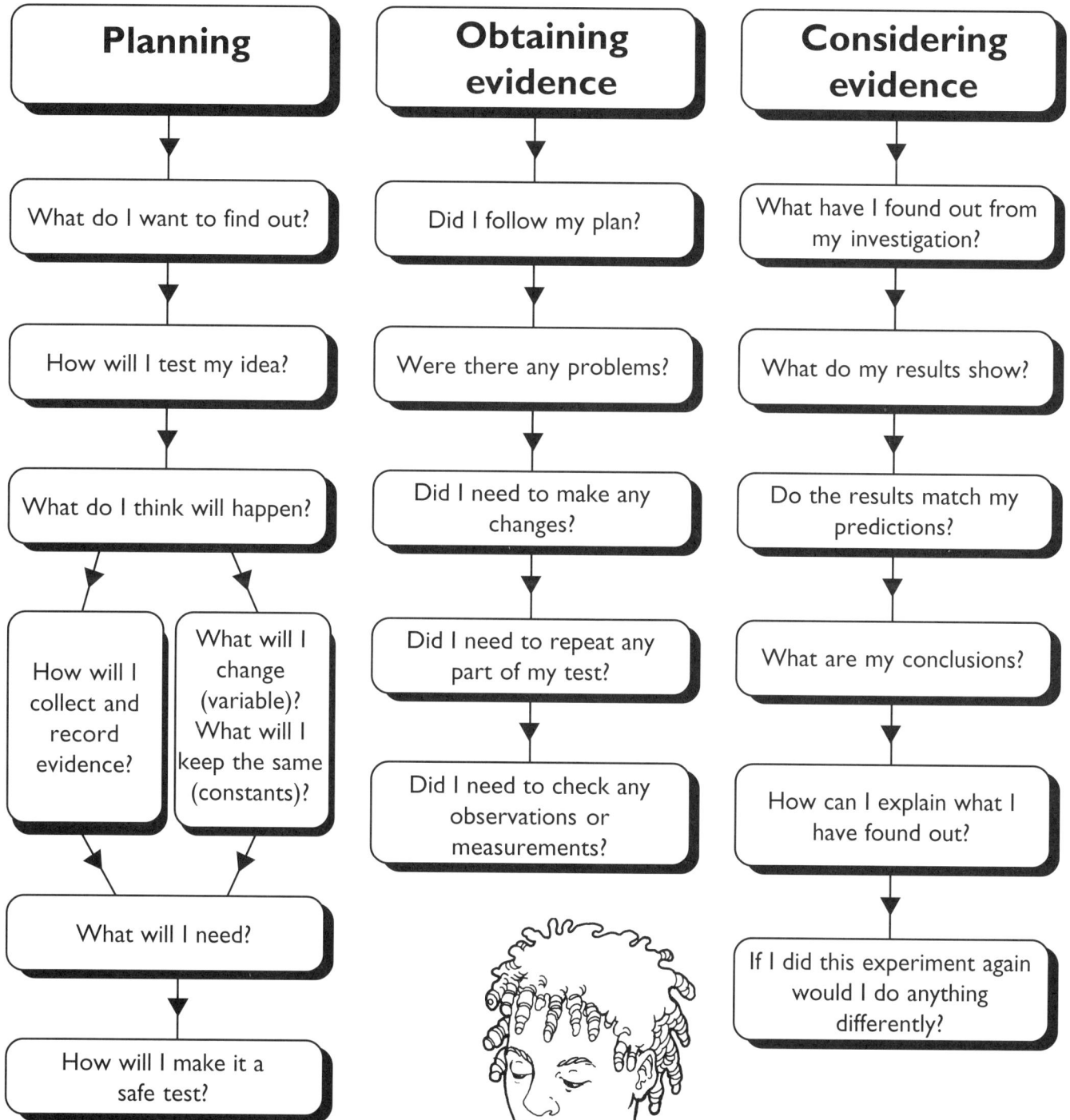

Planning

What do I want to find out?

⬇

How will I test my idea?

⬇

What do I think will happen?

⬇

How will I collect and record evidence?

What will I change (variable)? What will I keep the same (constants)?

⬇

What will I need?

⬇

How will I make it a safe test?

Obtaining evidence

Did I follow my plan?

⬇

Were there any problems?

⬇

Did I need to make any changes?

⬇

Did I need to repeat any part of my test?

⬇

Did I need to check any observations or measurements?

Considering evidence

What have I found out from my investigation?

⬇

What do my results show?

⬇

Do the results match my predictions?

⬇

What are my conclusions?

⬇

How can I explain what I have found out?

⬇

If I did this experiment again would I do anything differently?

Glossary

Air resistance (pp28, 36–37, 39) Force that slows an object moving through air.

Carnivore (pp4, 7) Any flesh-eating animal.

Circuit (pp44–47) Unbroken path that lets electricity pass.

Density (p32) The compactness of particles in a substance.

Detrivore (p4) Animal that feeds on the remains of plants and animals.

Displacement (water) (pp32, 35) When water is moved from its position by a solid floating or being immersed in it.

Dissolve (pp16, 18–20, 24) To mix with a liquid and disappear.

Food chain (p4) Series of organisms each of which is dependent on the next as a food source. Most food chains begin with a green plant.

Gravity (pp28, 30) Force that pulls things towards the Earth. It is this force that gives things weight. Other planets, moons and stars also have gravity. Their forces of gravity may be different from that of Earth. Gravity depends on the size of the planet.

Habitat (pp6, 9) Place where things live.

Herbivore (pp4, 7) Animal that eats only plants.

Micro-organism (p12) Living organism (e.g. bacteria, viruses) that is so tiny that it is not visible to the naked eye.

Molten wax (p25) Wax that has been made into a liquid through applied heat.

Pollutant (p20) Something that pollutes (contaminates) that which is clean.

Producer (pp4, 7) Organism that produces food from inorganic materials (e.g. photosynthesis); i.e. a plant.

Product (p24) Resulting substance after a change has taken place.

Respire (pp12–13) To take in air, change the gases in it and pass out the changed air.

Scavenger (pp4, 7) Animal that feeds on dead animals and plants.

Soluble (p16) Able to dissolve.

Solute (p16) **Dissolved** substance.

Solution (pp12, 16–17, 20, 23) Liquid with solid material **dissolved** in it.

Solvent (p16) Liquid that is capable of dissolving a substance.

Streamlined (p36) When a shape has a smooth shape to reduce resistance from, for example, air or water.

Turbulence (pp36, 38) Fluctuating flow of air or water.

Urban (pp8, 48) Relating to a town or city.

Vaporising (p24) Converting into vapour.

Variegated plants (p4) Plants that have leaves of two or more colours.

Voltage (p44) Potential of an electric current measured in volts. The volt was named after an Italian scientist called Allesandro Volta (1745–1827), who made many discoveries about electricity. Volt can be shortened to V.

Water resistance (p36) Force that slows an object moving through water.